ALL ABOUT DINOSAURS

TYRANNOSAURUS REX

by
Amy Allatson

KidHaven PUBLISHING

PHOTO CREDITS

Abbreviations: l-left, r-right, b-bottom, t-top, c-center, m-middle

Front Cover - metha1819. 2 - Kostyantyn Ivanyshen. 4 - iurii. 6 - robin2.
8 background - Photobank gallery. 10 - kridsada tipchot. 11 - JIANG HONGYAN.
12 - First Step Studio. 14 background - Alexandra Lande. 14 - DM7. 15 - Herschel Hoffmeyer.
16 background - Alexandra Lande. 16 - Elle Arden Images. 17t - Linda Bucklin.
17b - Sofia Santos. 18 background - Iakov Kalinin. 18l - MarcelClemens. 18r - guysal.
19 - Marques. 20 - metha1819. 22 - wawritto. 23 - nathapol HPS.
Images are courtesy of Shutterstock.com, with thanks to Getty Images, Thinkstock Photo, and iStockphoto.

Published in 2018 by
KidHaven Publishing, an Imprint of Greenhaven Publishing, LLC
353 3rd Avenue
Suite 255
New York, NY 10010

Designer: Drue Rintoul
Editor: Charlie Ogden

Cataloging-in-Publication Data

Names: Allatson, Amy.
Title: Tyrannosaurus Rex / Amy Allatson.
Description: New York : KidHaven Publishing, 2018. | Series: All about dinosaurs | Includes index.
Identifiers: ISBN 9781534521780 (pbk.) | ISBN 9781534521742 (library bound) | ISBN 9781534521667 (6 pack) | ISBN 9781534521704 (ebook)
Subjects: LCSH: Tyrannosaurus rex–Juvenile literature. | Dinosaurs–Juvenile literature.
Classification: LCC QE862.S3 A45 2018 | DDC 567.912'9–dc23

Printed in the United States of America

CPSIA compliance information: Batch #BS17KL: For further information contact Greenhaven Publishing LLC, New York, New York at 1-844-317-7404.

Please visit our website, www.greenhavenpublishing.com. For a free color catalog of all our high-quality books, call toll free 1-844-317-7404 or fax 1-844-317-7405.

CONTENTS

Words that appear like this can be found in the glossary on page 23.

WHAT WERE DINOSAURS?

Dinosaurs were **reptiles** that lived on Earth for more than 160 million years before they became **extinct**.

There were many different types of dinosaurs. They lived both on land and in water—and some could even fly!

WHEN WERE DINOSAURS ALIVE?

Dinosaurs first lived around 230 million years ago during a time called the **Mesozoic** Era. The last dinosaurs became extinct around 65 million years ago.

All land on Earth was together in one piece during the time of the dinosaurs. Over time, it has slowly split up into different **continents**.

WHEN ALL THE LAND ON EARTH WAS TOGETHER IN ONE PIECE IT WAS CALLED PANGEA.

PANGEA

TYRANNOSAURUS REX

Tyrannosaurus rex (tuh-RAA-nuh-sohr-uhs REHKS) was one of the biggest dinosaurs to walk the earth.

NAME	*Tyrannosaurus Rex* (tuh-RAA-nuh-sohr-uhs REHKS)
LENGTH	40 feet (12 m)
WEIGHT	9 tons (8 mt)
TEETH	60
FOOD	carnivore
WHEN IT LIVED	65 million–70 million years ago
HOW IT MOVED	walked on two legs

Tyrannosaurus rex became extinct around 65 million years ago. There are reptiles today, such as the crocodile, that look very similar to *Tyrannosaurus rex*. However, *Tyrannosaurus rex* is actually more similar to birds such as chickens and ostriches.

"TYRANNOSAURUS" MEANS "TYRANT LIZARD."

WHAT DID *TYRANNOSAURUS REX* LOOK LIKE?

Tyrannosaurus rex was around 40 feet (12 m) long and 13 feet (4 m) tall. Its head was a massive 5 feet (1.5 m) long!

We don't know for certain what color *Tyrannosaurus rex* was, but it's possible that it was green to **camouflage** itself in its **habitat**.

EACH TOOTH WAS UP TO 6 INCHES (15 CM) LONG, AND ITS BITE WAS AROUND THREE TIMES MORE POWERFUL THAN A LION'S.

WHERE DID TYRANNOSAURUS REX LIVE?

Tyrannosaurus rex probably lived in valleys that were covered with trees. The land these dinosaurs lived on is now North America. We know where *Tyrannosaurus rex* lived because we have found *Tyrannosaurus rex* **fossils** in these areas.

Tyrannosaurus rex could have lived in places other than North America, but their fossils haven't been found yet.

WHAT DID TYRANNOSAURUS REX EAT?

Tyrannosaurus rex was a carnivore. It hunted smaller dinosaurs such as *Triceratops* (try-SEHR-uh-tops). These dinosaurs were also **scavengers**. They would eat animals that had been killed by other dinosaurs or had died of other causes.

Many scientists believe that *Tyrannosaurus rex* ate up to 500 pounds (227 kg) of meat in one mouthful. This is about half the weight of an adult horse.

DINOSAURS LIVED ON EARTH 800 TIMES LONGER THAN HUMANS HAVE SO FAR.

WAS TYRANNOSAURUS REX THE BIGGEST DINOSAUR?

Tyrannosaurus rex was one of the biggest **predators** ever, but it wasn't the biggest dinosaur that ever lived.

The longest predator was *Spinosaurus* (spy-nuh-SOHR-uhs), which was up to 59 feet (18 m) long. It lived mostly in water, but like a crocodile, it could also live on land.

SPINOSAURUS

Brachiosaurus (brah-kee-oh-SOHR-uhs) was taller than *Tyrannosaurus rex*. It was more than 43 feet (13 m) tall. Scientists believe the tallest dinosaur was *Sauroposeidon*. This dinosaur was 59 feet (18 m) tall!

HOW DO WE KNOW...?

We know so much about dinosaurs thanks to the scientists, called paleontologists, who study them. They dig up fossils of dinosaurs to find out more about them.

FOSSIL

EGG

Scientists put together the bones they find to try to make the full skeletons of dinosaurs. From these skeletons, scientists can often figure out the size and weight of a dinosaur. We can also find out information about what it ate from its fossilized food and waste.

SCIENTISTS EVEN FIND FOSSILIZED EGGS AND FOOTPRINTS BELONGING TO DINOSAURS.

FACTS ABOUT TYRANNOSAURUS REX

IT WEIGHED UP TO 9 TONS (8 MT).

ITS TEETH GREW BACK AFTER THEY FELL OUT, JUST LIKE A SHARK'S.

IT COULD RUN AT A SPEED OF NEARLY 10 MILES (16 KM) PER HOUR.

ITS ARMS WERE ONLY AROUND 3 FEET (1 M) LONG.

DRAW YOUR OWN DINOSAUR

THINK ABOUT THESE QUESTIONS . . .

1. How does it move?
2. Does it live on land or in water?
3. What does it eat?
4. What color is it?
5. How big is it?

GLOSSARY

camouflage to hide or disguise in a habitat

carnivore an animal that eats other animals

continents any of the seven large masses of land on Earth

extinct to no longer be alive

fossils the remains of plants and animals that lived a long time ago

habitat where an animal lives

Mesozoic a period of time when dinosaurs lived from 252.2 million years ago to 66 million years ago

predators animals that hunt for food

reptiles cold-blooded animals with scales

scavengers animals that feed on dead animals

INDEX